Dinosaurs are split into two groups: Ornithischian (bird-hipped) and Saurischian (lizard-hipped).

Many prehistoric plants

Albertosaurus and Tarbosaurus were two large carnivores which had arms too short to bring food to their mouths.

Eoraptor is recognised as the oldest known dinosaur at 228 million years old.

Dinosaur eggs were first recognised in 1922 when fossilised nests of Protoceratops were discovered in the Gobi Desert.

To the Natural History Museum for all the wonder and inspiration it gave a small child, and to Arthur and his friends at Sherborne Preparatory School, Dorset for their off-the-wall ideas and the use of their fabulous library!

First published and distributed in the United Kingdom in 2008 by Ragged Bears Publishing Ltd,
14A Bennetts Field IE, Southgate Road, Wincanton, Somerset BA9 9DT.

Tel: 01963 34300 orders@raggedbears.co.uk www.raggedbears.co.uk

Reprinted 2012

Text copyright © 2008 Henrietta Stickland
Illustrations copyright © 1994 Paul Stickland
All other illustrations © The Natural History Museum, London
Designed by Karen Bale, Impulse Graphic Solutions Ltd
The moral rights of the author and illustrator
of this work have been asserted

A CIP record of this book is available from the British Library

ISBN 978 1 85714 383 6

Printed in China

Ragged Bears Publishing

DINOSAUR MORE!

By Henrietta Stickland

Original Dinosaur Roar!
illustrations by
Paul Stickland

A first
book of
DINOSAUR
FACTS

DINOSAUR ROAR! was written to introduce and celebrate the subject of dinosaurs for the very young - a bit of rhythmic, rhyming fun really! I discovered that nobody really knew what colour dinosaurs were, so it was a wonderful opportunity for the artist, Paul (Stickland), to let his dinosaurs come to life in a colourful way. Now, some fifteen years after the first publication of the book, I wanted to explore in more detail some of our favourite dinosaurs. I hope **DINOSAUR MORE!** will inspire all those budding young palaeontologists who are ready to start exploring the wonderful world of these extraordinary prehistoric creatures.

DINOSAUR TIMELINE

How many millions of years ago did dinosaurs live?

227		205		180		159	
Late Triassic		Early Jurassic		Middle Jurassic		Late Jurassic	

CONTENTS

Early Cretaceous

98

Late Cretaceous

65

DINOSAUR LONG

Diplodocus di-PLOH-de-kus

Meaning: *double beam*

Built like a suspension bridge, these improbably long creatures walked the earth during the Late Jurassic period. Huge muscles linked their pelvic bones to their tails. This helped them carry their tails off the ground. The length and size of the Diplodocus would make it very heavy, but part of the backbone was hollow, which would have meant that the Diplodocus weighed no more than two or three elephants.

Long, whip-like tail →

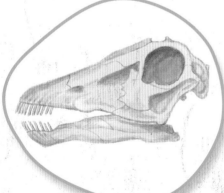

Scientists now believe their tails would have been carried in the air. There are no *fossil* remains that prove otherwise. →

DEFENCE

Like other *Sauropods*, the Diplodocus would have travelled about in herds - it's much safer being part of a group! Their only other *defence* was the whiplash tail and an ability to rear up and use their front legs.

SEE HOW BIG I AM

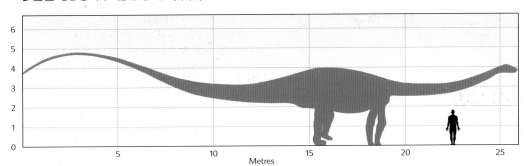

Metres

10 TONNES

Bulky body

Tiny head and small mouth with peg-like teeth

Walked on four columnar legs *(quadrupedal)*

Long neck

DIET

The Diplodocus was a *herbivore* and had to eat huge amounts of trees, ferns and other *vegetation* to keep it alive. The Diplodocus only had teeth at the front of its mouth so was unable to chew. Instead it had *gastroliths* that would grind up the *vegetation*. The ground-up food would then pass to another digestive area, where it would have been *fermented* down further by *bacteria*.

DINOSAUR FIERCE

Velociraptor vel-O-si-RAP-tor

Meaning: *quick plunderer*

This *ferocious* two-legged *(bipedal)* killer had large claws on its hind legs, with which it would attack its victims while holding on to them with short, strong arms. Only two metres in length, what the Velociraptors lacked in size they made up for with their *aggressive* nature. *Fossilised* remains have been found of this small meat-eater *(carnivore)* locked in battle with a much larger, horned dinosaur.

The Velociraptors hunted in packs, picking out ill, old or young victims.

SEE HOW BIG I AM

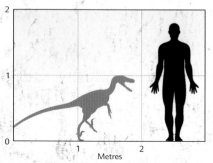

Metres

7-15 KG

DIET

They ate meat and stolen dinosaur eggs.

Three-fingered clawed hands

Approximately 80 very sharp, curved teeth, and a long, flat snout

A retractable claw on the middle toe of each foot was its main weapon

DEFENCE

Quick and sure-footed, and hard to outrun. Sharp claws and teeth were used in *defence* as well as attack.

DINOSAUR SPIKY

Stegosaurus STEG-oh-SORE-us

Meaning: *roofed reptile*

The Stegosaurus roamed the earth in the Late Jurassic period. They weighed about as much as a very large elephant, approximately two tonnes. The name Stegosaurus means 'roofed reptile', which refers to the rows of bony plates they had on their backs, necks and tails. It is thought that the bony plates, which were full of holes and grooves, allowed blood to flow through and control their body temperature. They were like prehistoric *solar panels!*

Large, flat, bony, triangular plates along its back

DEFENCE

The Stegosaurus was a very slow creature and could not outrun a *predator*. To defend themselves they would use their powerful tails, which were armed with vicious bony spikes.

Pairs of spikes at the end of the tail →

SEE HOW BIG I AM

Very small head with a tiny
brain and toothless beak

Walked on four legs *(quadrupedal)*,
but its back legs were twice as long
as its front legs

2 TONNES

DIET

**The Stegosaurus was a *herbivore*
and would mainly eat small shoots
and leaves, as they had very
small, rather inadequate teeth.
It is thought they had stones
(gastroliths) inside their
stomachs to help break
up tougher plants.**

DINOSAUR SQUEAK

Compsognathus   komp-soh-NAY-thus

3.6 KG

Meaning: *elegant jaw*

The Compsognathus was a small, agile *predator* that lived in the Late Jurassic period. One of the smallest dinosaurs, the Compsognathus would have ranged in size from a large chicken to a big turkey! *Fossil* remains of this dinosaur have been found in France and Germany, where, at the time this swift little mover lived, there would not have been enough *vegetation* to sustain larger plant-eaters which bigger *carnivores* existed on.

SEE HOW BIG I AM

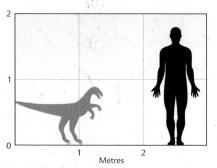

Metres

DEFENCE

Speed!

Small, pointed head and sharp teeth

Long, flexible neck

Three-toed feet with claws

12

DIET

The Compsognathus lived on small lizards, mouse-like *mammals* and insects. Like all dinosaurs built for running, Compsognathus had long back legs *(bipedal)* that really helped cover the ground. This gave it the speed needed to catch *prey*. It is thought that its streamlined shape would have made it much easier for Compsognathus to chase *prey* through the undergrowth.

DINOSAUR LUMPY

Ankylosaurus an-KIE-loh-SORE-us

4-7 TONNES

Meaning: *stiff lizard*

The Ankylosaurus lived in the Late Cretaceous period, some 64 million years ago. This 'armoured' dinosaur could be as long as ten metres, from its head to the tip of its strong tail, and was covered with oval-shaped, hard plates which were set into thick, leathery skin.

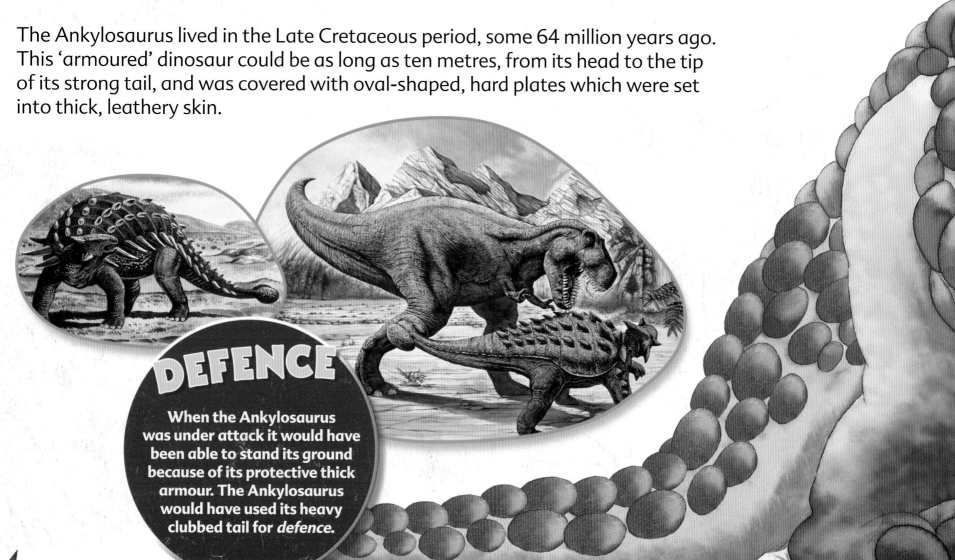

DEFENCE

When the Ankylosaurus was under attack it would have been able to stand its ground because of its protective thick armour. The Ankylosaurus would have used its heavy clubbed tail for *defence*.

SEE HOW BIG I AM

Bulky body with oval armoured plates

3
2
1
0
2   4   6   8
Metres

← Wide skull and a tiny brain

← Short neck

← Four short legs with toed feet (quadrupedal)

Unplated underbelly

DIET

As a *herbivore*, the Ankylosaurus would have lived on plants and low-growing trees. They would have needed a big amount of food to stay alive.

15

DINOSAUR ROAR

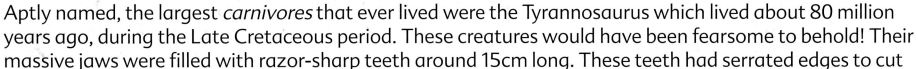

Tyrannosaurus tie-RAN-oh-SORE-us

Meaning: *tyrant lizard*

Aptly named, the largest *carnivores* that ever lived were the Tyrannosaurus which lived about 80 million years ago, during the Late Cretaceous period. These creatures would have been fearsome to behold! Their massive jaws were filled with razor-sharp teeth around 15cm long. These teeth had serrated edges to cut through flesh more easily. *Fossil* remains found in North America suggest that the Tyrannosaurus was about six metres tall and twelve metres long.

Large powerful jaws with long, sharp, conical teeth

Fingered hands with sharp claws and very short arms

Clawed feet

DEFENCE

Their size and ferocity were their greatest *defences*. The only *vulnerable* Tyrannosaurus would have been an elderly or ill one which could then fall *prey* to packs of smaller *predators* or *scavengers* such as the Deinonychus.

7 TONNES

Large eyes

Huge head

Bumpy skin

Long stiff tail

Long powerful legs (bipedal)

DIET

Flesh, and lots of it! The Tyrannosaurus was a deadly and efficient killer. Over short distances they could move much faster than their *prey*. It is thought that surprise attacks were how they operated, charging at their victim in a short burst of terrifying speed.

SEE HOW BIG I AM

Metres

DINOSAUR SLIMY

Apatosaurus ah-PAT-oh-SORE-us

Meaning: *deceptive lizard*

The Apatosaurus belongs to the group of *Sauropods* that includes the Diplodocus and the Barosaurus. The *Sauropods* were the largest animals ever known to have lived on land. The Apatosaurus existed in the Late Jurassic period.

They had five-toed hands and feet and a big fleshy heel. The *Sauropods* were in general so big that their arms and legs had to support the weight of about five elephants! What *Sauropods* had in common were very long necks and tails.

Like many dinosaurs they were herd animals, and would move around with their young close beside them.

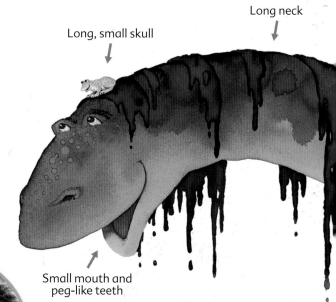

Long, small skull

Long neck

Small mouth and peg-like teeth

Long, whip-like tail

SEE HOW BIG I AM

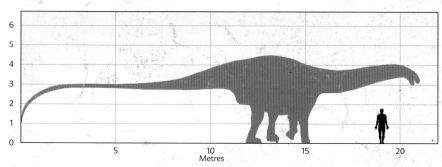

6
5
4
3
2
1
0

5   10   15   20
        Metres

DIET

Sauropods were plant-eaters (herbivore), and an adult would have to eat several tonnes of twigs and leaves every day to keep its huge body fed!

DEFENCE

Whilst stamping its heavy feet the Apatosaurus would use its long, strong tail as a whip to keep *predators* away.

30 TONNES

Bulky body

Four columnar legs
(*quadrupedal*)

DINOSAUR CLEAN

Iguanodon ig-WHA-noh-don

Meaning: *iguana tooth*

The Iguanodon existed in the Early Cretaceous era. They were a very successful species that *flourished* in large numbers. The Iguanodon owes its name to the fact that it had tall, ridged cheek teeth similar to those of the Iguana lizard that exists today. *Fossils* of tracks left by the Iguanodon show that they were capable of walking on either two or four legs.

DIET

A plant-eater *(herbivore)*, it had cheek teeth which ground the *vegetation* it ate. It is thought the Iguanodon would have bitten off foliage of lower-growing plants, such as horsetails and ferns, and chewed it with a sideways motion of the jaw.

4-5 TONNES

Toothless beak and tightly-packed cheek teeth

Four fingers plus a conical thumb spike

Legs much larger than the arms

Iguanodon could be either *bipedal* or *quadrupedal*

Three-toed feet with hoof-like claws

DEFENCE

Spikes on its thumbs were its best form of *defence*. If attacked, the Iguanodon could rear up and strike its attacker with this sharp weapon. It is thought the thumb would have been sharp and strong enough to *penetrate* its attackers' thick hides, or wound them in more *vulnerable* areas such as the eyes or throat.

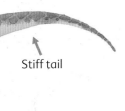

Stiff tail

SEE HOW BIG I AM

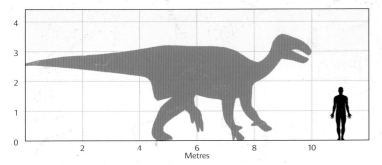

DINOSAUR SLOW

5.5 TONNES

Triceratops try-SERRA-tops

Meaning: *three-horned face*

Perhaps one of the most recognisable and liked of all dinosaurs is the Triceratops, which roamed what is now North America in the Late Cretaceous period. The Triceratops was the size of a very large rhinoceros, and rather resembled one too. It had thick, scaly skin, short sturdy limbs and broad feet to support its heavy body. However, unlike the rhinoceros, the Triceratops had a large armoured neck frill and three horns, rather than one. Its huge head made up one-third of the Triceratops' entire length!

Bulky, barrel-shaped body

DEFENCE

The Triceratops' sharp horns were an extremely good form of *defence*. It is thought that the neck frill could have acted as solar panels and certainly would have protected the neck and shoulders from predatory attacks.

22

SEE HOW BIG I AM

4
3
2
1
0

2 4 6 8 10
Metres

Large, bony frill with
pointed edges

Forward-pointing horns

Short, wide snout horn

Short legs with toed
feet (quadrupedal)

Toothless beak

DIET

These huge creatures
were *herbivores* and, like
the Iguanodon, could
chew well with its
cheek teeth.

DINOSAUR STRONG

Giganotosaurus gig-an-OH-toe-SORE-us

Meaning: *giant southern lizard*

The Giganotosaurus lived in the Early Cretaceous period and would have been even larger than the Tyrannosaurus, growing up to 12.5 metres long. At first *palaeontologists* thought that the Tyrannosaurus and the Giganotosaurus were related, but through further study they now know that even though there are lots of similarities between them, they were completely different animals - separated by huge geographical distances but also by around 30 million years *(see timeline on page 5).*

Up until 1994, when they found the first Giganotosaurus *fossil* remains, *palaeontologists* believed that Tyrannosaurus was the largest ever meat-eating dinosaur, but this find proved otherwise!

Clawed feet

DEFENCE

If you are a healthy, huge meat-eating dinosaur, with enormous sharp teeth, keen eyesight and the ability to run fast over short distances, you don't need to protect yourself from anyone - other than possibly your relations!

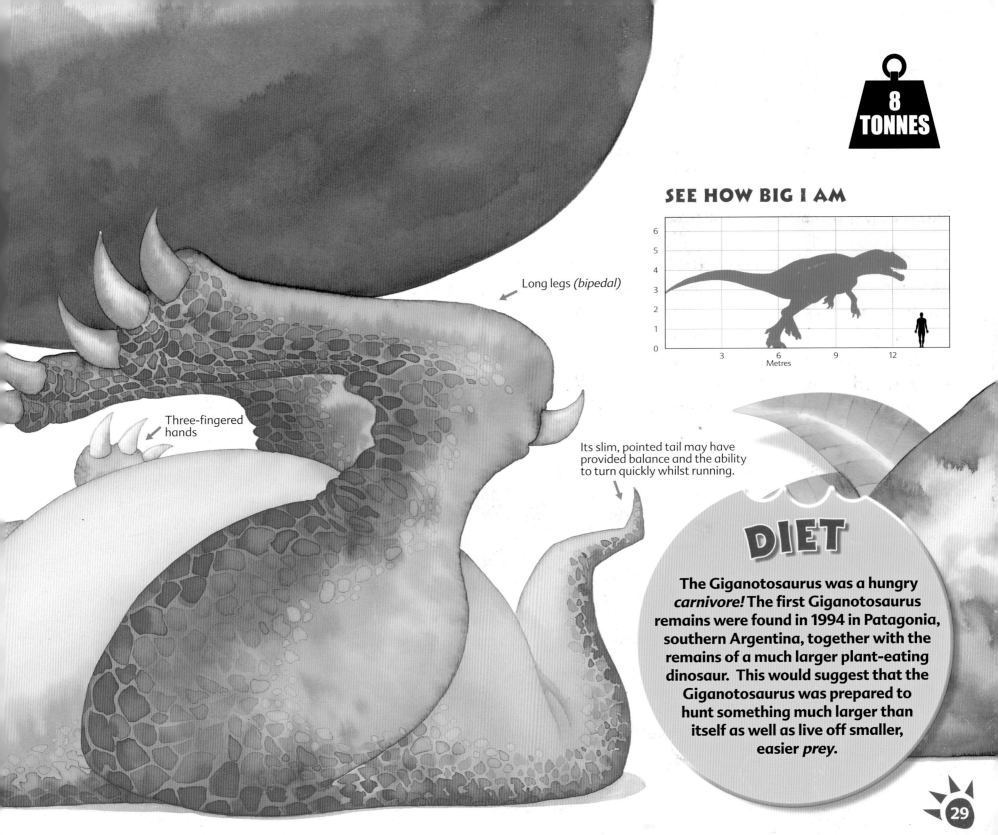

SEE HOW BIG I AM

Long legs *(bipedal)*

Three-fingered hands

Its slim, pointed tail may have provided balance and the ability to turn quickly whilst running.

DIET

The Giganotosaurus was a hungry *carnivore!* The first Giganotosaurus remains were found in 1994 in Patagonia, southern Argentina, together with the remains of a much larger plant-eating dinosaur. This would suggest that the Giganotosaurus was prepared to hunt something much larger than itself as well as live off smaller, easier *prey*.

GLOSSARY

aggressive
an aggressive creature is one which often attacks, or is easily made angry

bipedal
a bipedal creature walks on its hind legs only

carnivore
flesh-eating creature

defence
a means of resisting attack

ferocious
fierce or cruel

flourished
to thrive, to be successful

fossil
a relic or trace of a former living thing, preserved in the ground

herbivore
plant-eating creature

gastroliths
also known as gizzard stones, these stones are held in the stomach and are used to help grind up food

mammal
animal that suckles its young

omnivore
creature that eats both flesh and plants

palaeontologist
someone who studies fossils

predator
creature that attacks and kills other animals for food

penetrate
to force a way into something

prey
animal hunted or captured by another for food

quadrupedal
a quadrupedal creature walks on four legs

retractable
that which can be drawn up into the body (like a cat's claws)

sauropods
huge, long-necked, long-tailed, quadrupedal dinosaurs

scavenger
creature that looks around for, and lives off the remains of, other creatures' kills or eggs

solar panel
a panel of solar cells that absorb the sun's rays

vegetation
mass of growing plants

vulnerable
capable of being wounded; open to attack

INDEX

More Dinosaur Products from Ragged Bears

Dinosaur Numbers
£3.99 • 9781857143300

Dinosaur Opposites
£3.99 • 9781857143270

To see more of what
we do, to place an order
or to request a catalogue,
either phone 01963 34300
or go to our website,
www.raggedbears.co.uk

Dinosaur Fierce
£4.99 • 9781857143041

Dinosaur Roar!
£4.99 • 9781857143010

Dinosaur Colours
£3.99 • 9781857143294

Dinosaur Shapes
£3.99 • 9781857143287

Dinosaur Roar! Playing Cards
£3.99 • 9781857142969

Dinosaur Baby
£4.99 • 9781857143027

Dinosaur Slow
£4.99 • 9781857143034

Dinosaur Roar!
£9.99 • HB • 9781857142945
£6.99 • PB • 9781857142938

Dinosaur Roar! CD Package
£8.99 • 9781857143676

Dinosaur Roar! Colouring Book
£3.99 • 9781857143706

Ten Terrible Dinosaurs
£6.99 • 9781857142129

**Paul Stickland's
Book of Dinosaur Postcards**
£3.99 • 9781857142983

**Dinosaur Roar!
Activity Sticker Book**
£3.99 • 9781857142976

**Dinosaur Roar!
Hand Puppet**
£12.99 • 9781857141405

In 1992 a superb Stegosaurus skeleton was found which finally proved that their back plates formed two staggered rows.

The Triceratops' massive head was more than one-third of the whole length of its body.

Unlike many other creatures, the Tyrannosaurus' lower jaw was hinged halfway along so its could open its mouth extra wide - scary!

It is thought that the best armoured dinosaur was the super spiky Edmontonia.

A Tyrannosaurus tooth could grow up to 18cm (7 inches) long.

All dinosaurs laid eggs.